The Toothle

Written by Jonny Walker
Illustrated by Rupert Van Wyk

Collins

The toothless king of Bupkis Land chomped on pumpkins with his gums.

He cracked and gulped from ostrich eggs, and sucked on mushed-up plums.

"Cook! Come here!" the bad king said.
"Bring me shrimp in pots!"

I wish to be the biggest king, so you must feed me lots!"

5

Crimp the cook looked at the shelf.
His lips parted with shock.

"My lord, you chomped so much," said Crimp.
"I must go to the shop!"

"Grab my cash bag," yelped the king. "Spend all my cash on snacks!

Then bring them back, and stuff me full with crisps from mega-packs!"

Crimp spent the contents of the bag and filled a skip with food.

The bad king munched it up, but still it did not lift his mood.

"The food's all munched!" the king yelled out.
"So now what shall I do?"

I'm not the biggest king," he sniffed. "I'm foodless ... cashless too!"

"Come here now, Crimp!" snapped the king. "Kings must have full tums."

Crimp got munched as a second lunch!
The king just licked his gums.

Then he looked down at his beard and chomped a clump of hair.

He chomped and gulped, till all were left were gums upon a chair!

The king's food

19

Bad kings!

The toothless king of Bupkis Land is similar to this bad king.

This king upset a goddess.

He was punished with a never-ending hunger.

This king ended up munching himself, too!

F. Chauveau in et fecit

A big lunch

23

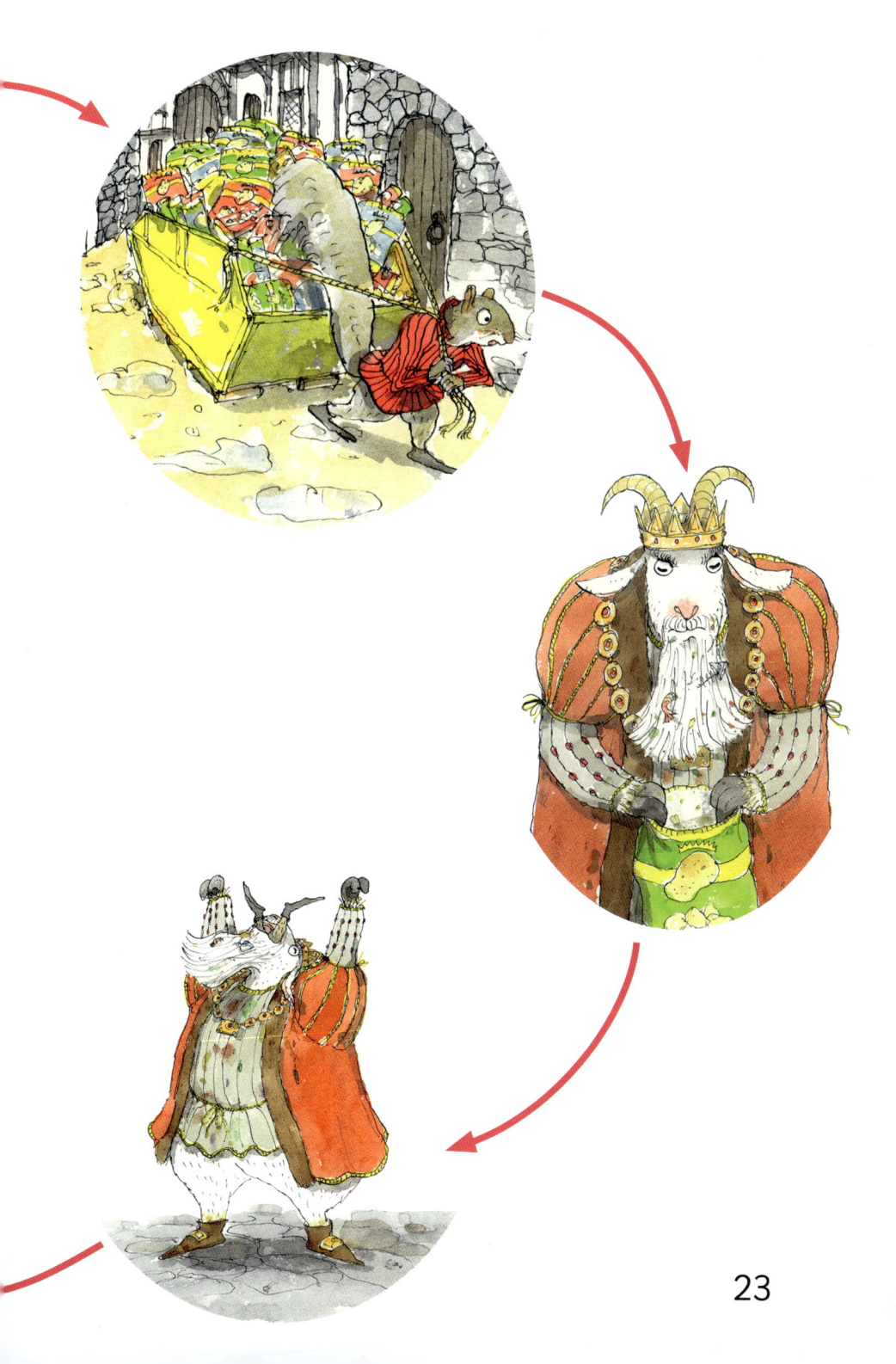

Review: After reading

Use your assessment from hearing the children read to choose words or tricky words that need additional practice.

Read 1: Decoding
- Turn to pages 8 and 9. Ask the children to sound out and blend **Grab**. (*g/r/a/b – grab*) Repeat for:

  spend (*s/p/e/n/d – spend*)   bring (*b/r/i/ng – bring*)
  snacks (*s/n/a/ck/s – snacks*)   crisps (*c/r/i/s/p/s – crisps*)

- Read pages 10 and 11 and focus on the word **lift**. Discuss its meaning in the context of the phrase **lift his mood**. (e.g. *improve, raise, make better*) Ask: How did the king feel before and after eating the skip full of food? (e.g. *sad, low, unhappy*)
- Bonus content: Turn to pages 20 and 21. Challenge the children to read the text aloud fluently, sounding any words they are uncertain of silently in their heads.

Read 2: Prosody
- Turn to pages 4 and 5 and discuss how to read verses in the poem. Focus on:
  o which words to emphasise (encourage the children to read page 4, emphasising alternate words for the rhythm)
  o the rhyming words (ask the children to read both pages, emphasising **pots** and **lots**).
- Ask the children to read both pages, keeping a beat and emphasising the rhyming words.

Read 3: Comprehension
- Talk about other humorous kings or queens the children have read about in poems or traditional tales. Ask: What happened in the end? How was it different to this poem's ending?
- Reread page 5 and focus on the theme of the poem. Ask: Do you think the author thinks it is good to be greedy and want to be the **biggest king**? What makes you think this?
- Turn to pages 22 and 23 and ask the children to retell the events, using the pictures as reminders. Challenge them to use interesting vocabulary, for example ask: What word could you use instead of "ate"? (e.g. *chomped, gulped*)